WITHD~~RAWN~~

MOON

MOON

POEMS BY DAVID ROMTVEDT

ILLUSTRATED BY RW SCHOLES

THE BIELER PRESS ☾ SAINT PAUL

1984

Designed by Gerald Lange.

Illustrations by RW Scholes.
Copyright © 1984 by RW Scholes

This project has been supported through a grant from the National
Endowment for the Arts in Washington, DC, a federal agency.

LIBRARY OF CONGRESS CATALOGING IN PUBLICATION DATA

Romtvedt, David.
    Moon: poems.

    1. Title.
PS3568.O5655M6   1984   811'.54   82-22812
ISBN 0-931460-14-x (limited edition)
ISBN 0-931460-16-6 (paperback)

The author would like to thank the editors of the following publications for permission to reprint poems used in this book:

American Poetry Review: Arson; Moon; This Window

The Arts: Last Night on Earth; Letter to William Stubbs on Uranus

Ascent: Man Up North

Aspen Anthology: Formal Setting; Tropical Madness

Chowder Review: Letter to William Stubbs on Uranus; This Could Be the World

Crab Creek Review: Gisenyi, Rwanda, Club Edelweiss

Fiddlehead: While Illegally Putting Garbage in an Institutional Dumpster a Man Thinks of Community and His Own Childhood

Ironwood: Albert Einstein and the Waves Rolling Into the Sea; The Men; Wanting; What If Flowers Were Gray and Smelled Like Rotting Meat?

Marxist Perspectives: Muraho Butare, Muraho Rwanda

Outlaw: In My Younger Days I Had a Dick Like Thunder

Paris Review: Pockets

Poetry Now: The Heavenly Mistakes Amid So Much Golfing

Raccoon: God; Last Night on Earth; Two New Trees in Our Field

Yakima: Thinking of Governor Ray's Position on Nuclear Power I Wonder If Calling Her Mad Would Be Slander; Meilleurville; Two New Trees in Our Field

The poem 'Moon' was first published as a broadside by the Graywolf Press, Port Townsend, Washington.

ONLY THIS

In 1984, when *Moon* was published, the people of the world faced daily the possibility of annihilation in a nuclear holocaust. The Soviet Union and the United States, the two dominant powers of the period, both possessed the weapons to destroy each other and the rest of the world many times over. Indeed, they possessed weapons that could end forever the earth's capacity to support life. The most important task facing all people was the creation of a world free of nuclear weapons.

I hope that by the time you read this note, that task will be accomplished and my words here will seem a little ridiculous, a little unreal. You will smile at this memory of fear and be shocked by the realization that nuclear weapons, so very ridiculous and unreal, were once a part of everyday life. Then I ask you to disregard this note and only read these poems as expressions of the human heart.

But if, when you read this, we are still sitting on the edge of nuclear war, then you must not only read the poems as expressions of the heart but you must also work to banish all nuclear weapons from the world. And one day to banish all human suffering. Only this.

—David Romtvedt, Port Townsend, WA

CONTENTS

for Lise Petrich

I open this window
and the wet air jumps.
Evenings the fog rolls up the road.
The stars grind into blurry sight.
Nothing could be important
and something is happening.
It seems like something is happening.

MISSING PARTS

ARSON

At work we found a rattler.
The job was to make a rip-rap
on the desert as if waves
would someday reach that sea. But it was
only to stop erosion so men could stand on artificial
mounds to fire their guns across the air. I don't
remember thinking the snake would strike. I can't
remember any fear or idea that I wanted
to take action. I didn't say a word when another boy
said, "We have to kill it" and no one disagreed. So we
did it with stones, at the end striking its head
like hammering nails to hold targets, hanging
on to the stone. Then an older man slit its belly
open, throat to tail, telling stories about other rattlers,
scrambled eggs and snake brains, being alone
on the desert. He uncoiled nine unborn snakes, eyes
still creamlike membrane. They tried to wind themselves
back round, moving from side to side. It may be they
were alive or if not, all tropism, some dead creature's
dance of nerve endings and light. I must not have asked,
must not have said a thing, just
looked, learning that rattlesnakes are born
one at a time: the unwinding of the young
on the flat surface of a stone
where they sizzle and pop in the faultless sun.

WANTING

A small boy stares at the sky.
For the bird he shoots in only his presence
the boy no longer exists.

The Berkeley Branch Bank of America no longer has any
    windows.
For the Mexican students shot in an open plaza
the windows slide up and down.

The gun is for a boy. The bird comes empty as the sky.
The bank is for itself. In Mexico there is music from every
    window.

You can see this. It is written in all the newspapers.
What you believe cannot change it being so.

The boy shoots, so there is eighteenth century physics.
    At ten o'clock
the bank doors open, the tellers stand in line.

As they incinerate the uncounted bodies
a small bird flying upward reaches the vault
of my head and hitting fast falls
dead. The boy leans on his gun.

THE MEN

Tomorrow they begin
blinding the men
to make them see.
The fresh colored
leaves will lie like paint
on the narrow streets, under their feet;
the open-eyed young men scraping
knuckles along walls.

In crowds walking together, brightly
clothed, often sloppy as the blind
will sometimes be, the part
in their hair maybe not right, now making sure
zippers always zipped. And nothing is impossible

for the blind men
to think about. They have lost
their last mirrored word: eyelid.

They will be opening department stores
for people and offering what people need.
Already the products are on display,
seen and shaped by the hands, held
and turned in the light.

I am beginning to understand
them, their slouch and hunch.
It does not take years standing up
straight or leaning over
to place a teaspoon beside a dish.

What difference does skin make anymore?
The men are not ruthless, they wash

with soap, they hammer nails and fill
file cabinets with yellow sheets of paper.

The Blind Drunk Man's Society though grows
noisier and later. No one
knows solitude in the meeting hall, their
new blue shirts, their blue woolen hats
over heads scraped clean. They are reminded
of the sky. Tomorrow they begin
covering the numbers on their doors, pretending
they don't know the street on which they live
or where it is. They will be as open
as a bathtub, they will cloud over
wherever they lie.

MAN UP NORTH

I'm biting my hands under a thick layer of reindeer hide gloves.
I'm southern and hot, brandishing a catalog of another gestalt.

They're blue, my hands.

Where is the Sunday afternoon drinking gang?

Adjusting the lantern with sticks dipped in dead whale,
a faint rose light on the sky with gold around the edges
and the butterflies or stars flapping through Orion. All of these

empty Schweppes bottles would make nice inlays for my icehouse
with their rich sounds and sense of a world that is missing.

I'm going bald like a sheet of music unplayed.
Neither over nor under talk make sense here with no other folk.

I'd gladly pluck out my heart if it'd get me to town where
I'd tell people I'm a tough old bird but I still make wishes:
a ride down a warm-water river, my ghost sprawled out on a chair.

I really am going bald and maybe blind though blind what
of it I make up the dancers in front of my eyes, make up
sandstorms to replace blowing snow, make up other hands
reaching for flesh...

I've got a bottle of caraway seeds, 10 lbs. of salt,
several liters of strong lager beer. I can dine
very well with a mirror propped up across the table
and say, "Hello, how was your day? I've made a nice Bröckel bread,
have you cut your lower lip? Or do you continue to pout?"

It's true, these hands are blue and a little bit stiff.

SOLSTICE

There was a pack of dogs.
Actually they were hunchbacked dogs.
They were foxes who thought they were dogs.
They were howling at the moon.
They were snarling at moose.

It was the longest day of the year
in Whitehorse, Yukon Territory. Three
meritless goats sat on top of a hill,
that is, a mountaintop, comfortable,
like cats in the crotch of a tree.

The mad dogs were winking at the rising sun.
In the south it was still night. Someone
said, "The light hangs like faded curtains."
That's the day's first moment, the moment
the day calls its own. "Mine," the day says.

Imaginary things were fading out of sight.
They were becoming unreal. Clean and bright
one could call Whitehorse. Whitehorse,
where in summer violin teachers
work twenty hours a day.

The earth may as well have been flat, turning
over and always the same. Night,
like the last piece of pie in a dish.
Warm hands reach for one more bit and lift
the pie, fragmented disc on the end of a string.

On lawns white neighbors set up tea
at almost any hour. People lie down
and look at the sky. Hungry for stars

they are like mad dogs howling under a lamp-post—
"Anything will do, or almost…"

As the sun rises, the movement of hands and feet,
that is, extremities, picking up momentum.
Again like hunchbacked dogs, now choking on steam.
At the pole silence and the idea of ice floes,
stumbling uphill away from the dawn.

WHAT IF FLOWERS WERE GRAY AND
SMELLED LIKE ROTTING MEAT?

He takes a lightweight
flexible pole and a length
of line to the woods where
he makes a special lure from
a canary feather, yellow and can turn
blue or green underwater and he throws it and
looks around and: gray... the summer is tied in knots.

The room is too warm, minor personal hysteria,
the cornea of a topless cage, another illusion and purposeless
joke, many hours of wan and enigmatic perusal.

Finally it is safe to go home! Everyone says.

With himself he takes a lovely
lightweight flexible pole and
a length of nylon
line. He goes to the woods
where he makes a perfect
special lure from a pigeon
feather, gray and can turn gray
or gray underwater and he lets it
fly and takes a breath and; meat,
rotting. Every shoe in the closet fills with candlewax.

I am a portfolio on its starboard side
is what he thinks and says
we are the most gifted of the defective,
delays have made past tense any suitable aspirations.

So he takes a pole, heavy and firm,
and fifteen feet of woven hemp to

the woods where he makes nothing, light
and colorless and the sinking moon, which
he only sees once and turns away or
twice and the flowers.

A FUNNY KIND OF AN ODE
FOR AN INTERSTATE SYSTEM

No one could possibly miss
the highway as it splits in two,
like a body split from crotch to face,
this town. When it reaches the river
the fish climbing to spawn look,
some imagine longingly, on the speeding,
the tractor-trailers like Grandfather Salmon.

I cross the bridge on foot and stop
to look down at the river
and the roadbed. The rain has ended
for this season. Broccoli leaves are collapsing
in the sun. Pea pods fall from drying
blossoms. No one I want stops on the bridge
to speak to me. I am the last walking man
or woman in sight. Only the police
busy themselves with this apparition. They
stop to chat, car full of radio and buzzing
what am I doing here? What am I doing
on the bridge now night? The auto
searchlight shines in my face. The stars
are incomparably grand and the fish
are alive. The shining light suggests
the cars, too, may be alive. Beautiful.
I wave my penis like the United Nations flag.
I should be home in bed listening
to the not so distant slap of rubber
on cement, secure that maybe I can
get anywhere from here. I shuffle
my feet to sweep dust onto the roadbed.

At home I sweep the floor with a wire broom.
Having crossed the bridge I sit down
to eat fried potatoes and drink quarts of light
American beer. It is simple food but nourishing
enough. The highway keeps on. The town
splits more and more in two. I listen
to the great peace of motors
and underneath my mind remembers
crickets and owls and plants that creak
in the night as they cool and unbend.

I can't see the moon for the streetlamp
above my window. The lamp is my moon,
rising deceptively at dark to fall like bombs
at daybreak. When the lamp goes down the sun
must be up and the highway. There are still horses.
They ride on the air-conditioned backs of trucks
and eat clover from galvanized pails. They saddle
their drivers and go on their way,
unclear memories of rocky trails
washed away or cliffs so steep they never
look down though maybe I do and see
the horsetrailer or a dead man and think,

shouldn't a dead man know more than we
who slide on our bellies from defeat
to gratifying defeat and wouldn't a dead man
let us know we were going about it wrong?

Blue trees tinged with gray. Green
opaque water. Back and forth, every day,
crossing the bridge. I pass over the highway
and the river and am passed by hundreds
of men and molecules of carbon monoxide

and flying insects in cars. I can't sit still
long enough to drive over the bridge, couldn't
reach around and touch the air so my feet
enclosed like snails in their shells slide
over the cement and metal expansion joints.

The traffic explodes. My hair flaps in the partial
vacuum of a logging truck. This is the only life
I can live, happiness is beside the point.
I am free as the salmon guided up ladders
and past hydroelectric generators. I go to spawn
with a half stiff erection and make
half live children. A few friends would be no help.
It's the highway no one could possibly miss
as it splits in two, like a body
from crotch to light blue face, this town.

THINKING OF
GOVERNOR RAY'S
POSITION
ON NUCLEAR POWER
I WONDER IF
CALLING HER MAD
WOULD BE SLANDER

By the chickenhouse
the visible stars,
the apple tree,
blossoms fallen and
what the chickens didn't eat
left white
on the ground,
the light
of the half-born moon
showing off
as the chickens,
too overfull of grace,
spin and creak
through this wreckage
of the idea of snow,
their tender combs and wattles
blistering in the glare.
One turns and another
looks. Sings. The
possibility that death
is the noisiest
experience of all
in a world
filled with noise.

I sit quietly
at a wooden table

by the wall
and envision a possible
apocalypse, the missing
chickens in the slow
burn of day.

————————————

Dixie Lee Ray is a
former governor of Washington
who strongly supported the construction
of nuclear power plants
throughout the state.

THE GENERAL

"We don't think we can't do it. You can't think negatively."
    —Bert Jones, Quarterback, Baltimore Colts

What I know about the Galapagos Islands
would fit inside the head of one small finch
600 miles from home or on the outside of one piece
of one batten from a sail of the Beagle
of whose owners I know nothing and maybe never will.
Still I am going to redeem that whatever-
you-think-it-may-be phrase at the top of the page.

It's about stress. About how much any one creature
or aggregate of creatures can or cannot do. About
stress. In times of stress it is best to relax,
get enough sleep, take enough juices, remember
there are many things that must be gotten through.

Sometimes you will think perhaps you
think you cannot do it. I can't
do it, I hope you are able to scream.
Then there are harder things to come.

Don't be anxious. Now I'm getting to the General's
daughter, wading in up to her crotch, all flashing
teeth and foaming thighs, the mountain she climbed.
The General's husband, famous for his role breaking
role, up to his crotch in orange jello, sort of sneering
into the camera to let it be known how
he feels no one knows. The General herself,
famous not for redefining
what ought to be done, what position
might be taken, how this life will be lived,
not for any such stuff, but famous,

for doing what men have always done,
just as well as men have done it,
being a General, not changing at all.

That's the end. Not that it should
come right there at that point
but I do what I can. Don't think I don't
think I can't do it, whatever
the hell that means. So.

OVERFLOW

Even in nothing there is too much.
A drop of water, clear, a hole in the sky.
On the other side of a window
or looking out at you from a mirror.
This is nothing too much.

Even darkness the greatest of nothing.
The empty space between two days.
The stomach waiting for food. The inside
of an empty aspirin bottle closed up
in a paper sack and thrown on a truck.
All this even is nothing.

Like the eyes of a hyena,
no pupils, no iris, no whites.
Eyes like nothing
look into nothing and back out.

Putting on shoes to take a walk.
Taking off shoes to look at feet.
A pebble? A beetle between the toes?
But there's nothing. Inspect the feet.
Shake the toes. Red dust
fills the air, particles of earth,
broken clay which breaks in turn and spreads
the light. The light crashing into bushes
and trees, crashing into buildings,
crashing through dark glasses,
this light.

I am looking for small things, the one
chipped aspirin tablet in the bottom
of the bottle, the hole left

when a nail fell out of the heel
of my shoe, now filled with mud,
now dry, a single red flower or yellow
flower, an unopened box of cigars,
a man who doesn't know he's alive. I grin
and say, "Here is something insignificant."
Here is something small enough to hold
in a hand, something to throw away.

Traveling I see nothing
in the aisles of a train, riding
on the roof of a bus, loading
a rifle with bits and pieces
of notes from the dead, or in myself
in Lubumbashi, Shaba, where I've never been,
reading novels about secession, looking
at buildings and streets, lying in bed
listening to termite wings, falling.

My hands fly from face to feet
to crotch to face to sides and fall.
At the very least, enough.

I dream of a lake
without fish, a tree without fruit,
men who chase birds from the sky with explosions
and put fish in lakes to pull them back out,
who harvest crops to feed their families.
Such men, such lakes and sky, such trees.

When I wake in a room the ticking of a clock,
salt on a table, a clod of dirt polished
smooth from turning and turning.
Chicken bones, cat bones, buffalo bones, little
splintery damned bones of a fish, word bone.

Door and lock and key. Trunk. A tiny scar
on the back of a thigh, bells ringing in ears.
A submachinegun, a cup of tea.

All morning, puking and roaming, eyes sewn open,
spitting up mud and shitting blood. I'll
tell you what I'd like, just once,
a thing not too much, a thing enough,
a rope and a wing, a pyramid,
maybe the loss of an eye.

FAR AWAY

MESSAGE FROM ZAÏRE

I can say in good faith that I am not
an ax-murderer, rapist, mercenary.
I am white in Africa, sometimes
a crime, sometimes we let the dead
stay dead. Me, I'm alive. The sun
shines everyday. Once a week I'm feverish
and lay myself down to dream of fir
trees and wet snow pushed up on sidewalks.
The water is teeming with life,
unplanned, it's out to get me.

Early in the morning the trees repose
and the corbeaux make ground beef
out of the air, sending songs back
to North America, where their all black cousins,
Crow and Raven, await the word,
this white-breasted message from Zaïre.
The air wakes up and dribbles
out around the leaves concentric circles
from here to there until me
who starts breathing and remembers
the past, telegram on a knife.

MEILLEURVILLE

Those of us who move around
in certain ways must
try to keep alert.
There is no time for growing vegetables.
We are barely able
to pick wildflowers along the road.
Some of us get lost
or disappear. Some of us,
we think, get disappeared.

There was a bar where we went.
The soldiers lay face down, both
the talkers and the dancers moved
around them. There was another room
ankle deep in piss where we stood
on cement curbs and passed
our beery news wherever
there was space.

It is like that here. Sometimes
people we didn't know knew us
would call out our names.
That too happens here. I have
not seen any children. I hear
they are brought as a kind
of tool. Some will use
any tool to find what they
think they need to know.

People where you are must
still be moving around. That is good.
Here we move in small spaces.

Some of us even manage
to move a great deal.
Each morning I move my fingers
a certain number of times.
One, two, three, I count
the mountains near your house
where we used to walk.

Now I have a bad foot.
It is not serious. At least
no one seems concerned.
A man who asked after my health
has disappeared.
Let's say he is traveling.

If you know where I am
do not be in a hurry
to pay a call. When that happens
it will be soon enough
not that I won't wrap
my arms around your body
and listen to our two hearts
pumping blood. I will.

One thing
I used to like about traveling
was the wind blowing
on my face, my nose
always red and peeling
from being burnt. Now
I have to close my eyes
in full sun those few days
when it is out, not often.
The sun isn't out often.

Still my nose reddens and peels.
Whenever I am in the sun
it is very hot. I haven't
much sense of time
but it must be hot here
almost year round and I'd say
I can smell citrus, orange or lemon,
never mango or papaya or pineapple.

This must be a desert
to which men have brought water
and crops. How like a detective
a traveler must often be.
There are very few birds
and no clouds in the sky.
Of course, as I said,
I am seldom out.

Even so these observations
can't be simple chance
and just as a lizard may come
clicking across the stones
so maybe one day you
will arrive and like travelers
stopped along the road
we will speak of making up
what we have lost, what
even casual travelers in their haste,
call lost time.

THE RWANDAN POST OFFICE
COMMEMORATES WORLD LEPERS' DAY

Being a phantom people stare.
They have taken away existence and stare.
I like to say we have come
from what we have survived on
and keep on moving.

This time next week I could be
the last walking white man in Butare,
buying ivory rings made from the bones of a cow.

The people both stare
and observe their staring
at the same time.

The whole scene is the scene
I remind the old Mama, bargaining.
She smiles, "A young man
is not necessarily a foolish man."
I did not weave the clothes I wear.

On the stamp Albert Schweitzer is smiling
in his special disembodied way.
A piano keyboard hangs on the horizon
with 22 keys, part
of one bar of the score
for Toccata is hammered up above
the keys. Albert S. smiles
because it is World Lepers' Day.

GISENYI, RWANDA, CLUB EDELWEISS

The bird sings it's own song
in whatever tree it sits. Hands are raised
in gratitude for peace. Roads are built
for the owners of imported automobiles.

Much of the year people look at the sky
and hope for rain.
There is no rain. The tragedy
is not that we are sick and poor
but that some wish us sick and poor.

If there is no place for something
it is buried or transformed.
If we have no bed
we sleep on the floor.
If we have no house,
the ground.
Those who have shoes wear them.
If there are windows
they are opened. The air
drifts through the house. The light
illuminates our faces.

A drunken man once tried to destroy the garden of a European.
He ran ripping out beans, bananas, groundnuts, yams,
even weeds and poisonous plants.

The priest goes about on a bicycle.
He blesses people
who are too sick to go to the Mission.
He tells the doctor
where to find the sick.

The word for goat's milk is amahenehene,
for sheep's milk, amatamatama.
Given the number of people
who have tasted either of these things
it is a triumph of hope to have the words at all.

People walk to the market on paths
or next to new roads in long trails like ants,
baskets on their heads and backs.
Some have nothing to sell and no money
with which to buy. They trade
for rice and soap and beans. They loiter
along the paths talking to strangers.
Some pretend to be well-to-do-town-dwellers.

The bed for the dead is called ikiliba.
The dead themselves are called ikiliba.
Ikiliba carrying ikiliba.

Of all the birds
we are most fond of the small colorful ones,
like the wagtail and weaver.

WHILE ILLEGALLY PUTTING GARBAGE
IN AN INSTITUTIONAL DUMPSTER
A MAN THINKS OF COMMUNITY
AND HIS OWN CHILDHOOD

It's hard to say what belongs
to whom. Where, for example, one group's garbage
starts and another's leaves off. Memory
too is hard to own. A young boy

playing in hay piled high in a barn
slips and falls out past a block and tackle
landing on the back of a holstein cow.
The boy is the other, the self never falls.

Or like a bad dream running along
behind the cows as they line up
to be milked, a concrete trough
sloping down to carry away shit and piss.
Running across the holding yard
I slip on a board and fall into the ditch.
I smell like a dream.

Later learning to drive, coming down a hill
on gravel, not knowing the brakes or the clutch
and into another ditch. Our dog in the back
slides and is pinned breaking her hind legs.
Rushing to get out I slip on the running board
and again I fall, then back up
and the dog heals.

On the way home from church
Grandpa died in the car
with a piece of fruit in his hand

and when we stopped he too fell
forward like dogs and boys.

Now the grown man,
holding a sack becoming compost, looks
at his knees that shake and remembers
all these things. He feels himself falling
but hangs onto the dumpster, thinks of community
and sniffs at the law.

IN MY YOUNGER DAYS
I HAD A DICK LIKE THUNDER

In my younger days
I had a dick like thunder.
In my days with Gisela
she said I was such a spurt.

We would pay 12 rand
to stand in line at the Gretchen
near the airport, row on row
of cars marked Hertz,
then leave in Gisela's Ford
Scorpion to Durban for the weekend,
her hand in my crotch, driving.

From the Gretchen all the way
down Munster Straat,
the two of us singing, "We're
the have-its sailing through life."
Our worlds pressed in around each
other. Well, if the poor
get a leg up on the car
I'm undone, she smiled.
My erection sank.

GOD

God is not the poem.
The poem is not God.
What is apparent may be good or may not.
When it's cold it's cold.
Don't think of the day when it may be hot.
When young men grow orange trees inside particle accelerators.
Think of God.
Think of the poem.
Orange trees made of glass break up under pressure.
Blood flows.
Glass spins up into young men's heads.
Mouths full of glass, brains full of glass, eyes and nose firing
    glass in bursts...

God is no poem.
God is a white man humping a buffalo, a black man walking
    underwater.
God is certain women.
God is no poem.
No poem is no God.
These two things are mutually beneficial to the mutual exclusion
    of each other.
Don't think of the dead.

It is not hot out.
It is not Sunday.
Borders are crossed.
Accept pressure.
Accept blood flowing through veins or across open systems.
What is good may be apparent, maybe ultimately.
What is not young need not be old.
Rest and wait. God is no poem.
Question.

Think of the poem.
Lyric on lyric on lyric across borders.
Particles spin off under pressure.
Lyric turns romance turns tragedy turns gothicsciencefiction-
    pornography.

White man humps buffalo.
Yellow woman carries mucous in a leather bag at her waist.
Holy mucous.
Holy buffalo.
Holy white man spinning off into particles.
Brown Grandmother patting round tortillas to fry up and eat.
Red teenage male patting round red teenage female ass.
Orange trees under glass.
Today is cold and tomorrow is cold.

God is no poem.
No poem talks to God.
We are glad for what we have.
We are glad for what we have.
We are glad for what we have.
It is not matter, not belief.
There simply is no God here to speak of.
Here he comes now.
Yes, here she comes now.

TROPICAL MADNESS

The guitar sways in the trees, leaves rest
motionless and the wind blows, notes
are all over and lizards weave rythmically
as they run for their dinner, these notes.

Then they sing. The jolly pastels on my shirt
laugh and leave. I am left in solitude wearing
a white suit and I am out of gas. Petro Zaïre
has turned off the pumps, closed the doors
and gone home to no dinging bells
or gone to a bar where the music
is a pile of pick-up sticks gone nuts. I am not,
nuts I mean, and there are no clouds scudding
across a greasy sky. The bus leaves for town
and it's a sound videotape with geese and pregnant
goats. The driver smiles and hands me a ticket.

This proves I've been where I'm going
or it proves the symphony's in town. By the window
the dust flails and the audience vomits
as we pass. They laugh when I mention
the guitar and the corn beginning to grow
on the experimental farm in Shaba. Up north

12 expert agronomists regard the fields and cache
their plane tickets home in the UN flag. 12 guys
tapdancing on corn seeds disguised as brains.
The people are still in training. They may not
vomit quite as much now though they still know how.

Things are encouraging. Afternoons I traverse
the lake, make the fish jump. They figure

the noise I make with my nose is no worse
than the splash re-entering water. They nibble.

I snap. The guitar is on strike against nature.
That leaves the leaves to give up all the music
there is in this half-cooked climate. A few more

minutes and the sun itself will set and the wind blow.
Dusk becomes night. Everyone's out dancing. And
it's lucky each day at last finds its own pure end.

MURAHO BUTARE, MURAHO RWANDA

Though I'm not happy to wait I wait
until five o'clock when I sit down
and order a beer—a Primus, 57 francs
in the Hotel Ibis and he says, "It is impossible."
There is no Primus. So I get up
from my low slung chair and move down
the street to the Faucon, the other
hotel, owned by the same old
Belgian family but where the clientele
is local and small time. I'm happy
to sit down at five past five and order
a beer, a Primus, even if it's not
so cold as up the street. There's no
power here and the generator's
over there. At 5:30 I have another
and sit. The air, though full of dust,
is good enough. I can't see the houses
on the hills. In front of my eyes they ride,
Arabs and Africans and Europeans,
on their splattering two-cycle machines.

Maybe someone sees me and shakes
my hand, bends his mouth, sits down.
It's six o'clock and we order a Primus.
The lights would come on if there were any power
but there isn't so they turn on
the candles and I can hear the generator click
at the Ibis and the crowd breathing and ice
oozing around in glasses of gin.
Maybe whoever comes gets up to go home
to his dinner or idea of fun. The night
is blacker than the faces around me. I'm
the moon in this sky, sucking up light

coming off dark. I'm jumbled. People
never give up looking at me. They don't
scream anymore. They're tired. Half
of them are still servants, most of them
couldn't speak to me if they wanted.
We're settling in now and if we're not friends
we're not exactly enemies.
It's not worth the trouble hating each other.
Life isn't long, there are a thousand hills,
a house on every hill, never too far to walk.
There's always a candle and the man
brings another Primus like a star
in no hurry sits on the sky.

---

*Rwanda is a small country in Central Africa. Butare is a
town in that country. Muraho is a formal greeting in
the Rwandan language.*

THIS WINDOW

I was thinking of Antonio Gramsci in Montreal, a star,
clambering up the wide stair to a hypothetical apartment,
remembering those years in prison, perspiring, finally
being able to rest in his own good chair.

He looks out over the rue Hutchison
or across to his desk where there is a terse note
from Lenin: Antonio, when the time comes the capitalist
will sell the hangman the rope.   —Vladimir Illich.

I would say that is true and later, Antonio,
we do not think the world is obscene,
God is no shithead and the true yellow sun
shines through fog, sometime window to the next world.

LAST NIGHT ON EARTH

MOON

If you are are a man
who loves women please now look
at the nipples of the woman you love.
Turn to her in this very moment and begin.
Do you think a poet or anyone else
for that matter can say that a nipple
is somehow like a moon, say that
nipples swell and rise like dark moons?
I think not. Nothing is really like
nothing else. In beginning
some of you will want to tear her shirt open.
I will say to nonviolently unbutton
her shirt but that is my personality.

Look at her round nipples. If your lover
is not here or if you have no lover ask
the woman seated nearest you if she would
like you to look at her nipples. She may
say no. Do not press the issue, perhaps
you will sneak a glance when she doesn't see.

If you are a woman
who loves women look at your female
lover's nipples. Ask her to look
simultaneously at your own. You will
notice each others' breasts. Let your
four nipples touch. Do not think
the four breasts are any more four moons
than your four nipples. You may be envious
of your lover's large breasts if they are large
or of her smaller breasts if they are that.
Remember we are here addressing nipples
so do not let breasts distract your attention.

The two of you can look at each other in mirrors
or upside down or in showers. If you are now
beginning to show your nipples to your lover
please do not be angry with the lonely man
who sneaks a glance your way.

　　If you are a woman
who loves men that too is alright. You
can look at your own nipples or you can
look at the man you love as he looks
at your nipples or you can look at
the man's nipples for they will harden
and rise. And just as your nipples are not
like moons so his are not at all
like cold nickles and dimes.

If by some sad and cruel blow of fate
your male lover has no nipples and you are disgusted
by the narcissistic pleasure of yourself you may
go and look at the moon rising, trying
to look only at the moon. Now I have come to that
for which some of you have been waiting.

　　If you are a man
who loves men, you who some will call
cursed, who in some way many do not
understand are blessed, you too must now
open your shirts to each other groping along
in the way you do. Like everyone else
you have no parts like moons, you are, of course,
nothing like nothing else. We are all here
together now, I hope, with our shirts in our hands.

TOGETHER

Elisabeth walking in the woods with Ann,
says Ann is showing her where to walk the dogs,
how to make sure one or the other
doesn't run away. But really Ann is alone
and a voice in her head is telling Elisabeth,
Ann is showing you how to be alone.
Don't say anything, pay attention, you
can learn how to be alone.

It is the way Ann walks,
the things she notices, that
the world expands around her like a leaf
and Elisabeth feels herself disappearing
into the world. Ann is sending her on a voyage,
teaching her how to be alone.

At home Elisabeth thinks about this—about
a relationship with a man now severed. For her
making love is good, she wants to make love, she says,
but then the other night she didn't want.
The man, once her life,
came and they tried to make love
but Elisabeth felt only a sickness in her stomach
and a desire to say no. No, I don't want.
She said nothing.

Now maybe she doesn't want to make love with anyone
except herself. Ann is teaching her how to be alone.
Elisabeth is learning to like what she learns.
Maybe in one year or two she will be able
to be with a man again, maybe, a man
who will have waited for one year or two, maybe.

TWO NEW TREES IN OUR FIELD

for Annie Lou Romtvedt, 1892–1965

I want to say this world
is as beautiful as you
with your legs that walk,
two thick stumps that cross the fields,
and your branches and leaves.

If there is a bird you are like
it is no small twittering thing
but large and calm and hard at work.
There is no bird I know severe enough
to be likened to you.

More like the cows
who gave you milk or the cows become
more like you, crossing the fields.

At night or in a spare moment
I remember Sondre, husband, reduced
to sitting with a cushion for his poor bony ass,
talking about fiddle music, shouting
10,000 Swedes came out of the weeds
chased by one sick Norwegian. Old Sondre,
the one sick Norwegian of his dreams,
stealing sugar and salt which you knew.
He died on his 160 acres, no gift
from the government long ago
after all the work. And you going on.

Now nobody much remembers the language.
We think we are Texas more than Norway,
cottonwood trees more than distant steep fjords.

You too die on the place, the 160 acres,
and stay where you are, planted
with next year's hay. You, Grandmother,
like the spirit of vetch or alfalfa
rooted in the land, a spirit I know
who doesn't fly away like no bird
on wings of sky, because of you
and where you stay with your two great
stumps of legs and our field
with two new trees.

POCKETS

This pair of pants has four pockets.
It can be seen how lovely they all are
carrying their duty-free cargo and passing
through every door they come to. They
go everywhere the pants they are attached to
go. It would be silly to do otherwise,
make a break for it, as it were.

Sometimes as the pants go through a door a hand
takes from the pockets a ticket. Rarely
do the pockets find themselves well acquainted
with these tickets. The hand takes the ticket,
holds it for a moment, then passes it on
to another hand which, again, rarely covers
the ticket with the close darkness of a pocket.
Even more fantastic would be pretending
the pockets ask themselves about these tickets.

If the pockets are not full there is room
for the hands alone. Sometimes the hands
are like glass, that is they are stiff or they
are cold or they shatter and settle, many
small pieces in the bottoms of the pockets.
Then the pockets are cocoons and the hands
later come crashing loose flapping their fingers
like some goof ball moth the pockets have never seen.

Legs and feet are important to pockets too, for without
these there would be no pants and pockets would find
themselves tacked solely on breasts or sewn boldly
on the side of a bicep, to be used as no more
than a cigarette holder or waiting room for greasy combs.

Yes, this way the pockets roll carelessly across
the earth, pass through air or water or anywhere
else the pants can think to go.

THIS COULD BE THE WORLD

I'm very glad to be here. My eyes open and close,
my hands make circles in the air, the air
is in most places still breathable and will sustain
life for which I can give no thanks to the ethical bankruptcy
called capitalism which I am unable to mention
over the whirring of the engines.

I'm afraid there is no sweet blue sky left.
And the cosmic consciousness is out to lunch.
What I see really could be it. Here is the oddest answer
yet given to the energy problem: burn eucalyptus.

13, 12, 11, 10, 9, 8, 7, I can go no farther.
I'm told not mentioning something can mean it isn't there.
The less economics is mentioned the more it seems to be there.
I've hardly mentioned it at all. I think some people think
people are more important than birds and that it is a good idea
to purchase land as an investment which means that the land
is subdivided and then it dies and so forth.

If there is a sweet blue sky left I certainly hope
it's the sweet blue sky of possibility.

Still I'm glad to be here.

This opening and closing of the eyelids,
once thought to be the analysts' war of the worlds,
is now known as the body's desire
to be everywhere at once or the faucet's leak
into the brain's fuzzy basin. We know this
as well as we know a lot of things.

I, who sometimes fart while sleeping and wake myself up,
who look forward to opening my eyes again quite shortly,
hope, for the foreseeable future, to have the complete use
of my ears. Red roses would please anyone
who has been on a deserted street, no people
shouting to beat the band, the empty windowboxes
waving their flags, the tiny streets coming together.

Years have gone by. As far as I know
nothing else can happen. Even in radios there is the idea
of wisdom and some things are worth believing in
though one of those things is not beauty queens
still there are other things
for which I am glad enough to be here.

FORMAL SETTING

Someone has left a silver spoon, or stainless steel,
lying on a plate, then someone has left a room.
A spoon, alone, begins jumping on a plate,
leaping in air like a bean,
until with a clatter a plate breaks.

Seated on the toilet someone is evacuating its bowels
while a spoon is lying on a table made of wood.
A spoon is tired but begins again to leap
while there is still time and finding a second
wind a spoon is coming down hard
for minutes or hours or days when
a table relents and falls in many small pieces
to the floor. The floor lets free an anticipatory
hum. Overcome by the longing for knowledge
a spoon begins a third time its hulking pirouettes.

Someone, having finished, flushes a toilet
and listens to the rasping liquid and waste.
Were it not for this
surely somone would feel a change.

The floor is beginning to vibrate like a string.
Oh, a spoon does not know what is possible
and not possible in this world, jumping on.
And the floor moans and sags to the ground.

You would think someone would have
some small glimmer of perception but no
someone is inspecting its chin in a mirror
while the earth itself unfolds and a spoon,
at its center, is carried away like soup.

Someone, opening a door, at last wonders
what has been going on and sitting down
to an empty plate asks where it can be
someone could have left a spoon.

THE HEAVENLY MISTAKES AMID
SO MUCH GOLFING

And then the wind, the angelic turn signals.
The children play games, Forget-
Me-Not, Famous Functions, Electro-hoop,
and turn it over in their collective mind:
the animals because they move.
No, the plants because they don't move.
But if it's the other way round?
Then the plants still, because they move.

The old people, who watch from the patio
and who will all be dead by this time next year,
don't understand and lie down flat along
the surface of the house. One child
picks a dandelion but the plant stays rooted.
The child stands there holding a stemless blossom.
One old woman says, " I'm bored silly,
and can only
                remember
        one Sunday   in my entire life—

the Sunday I was

                out
                chasing
                        butterflies
                with Jacob Walsh
                                who caught
a giant monarch and had a tremendous erection..."

The children pay no attention.
The older people actively pay no attention.
At some point there is golfing.

LETTER TO WILLIAM STUBBS
ON URANUS

Well, this morning I went waltzing
(a sort of a dance the people here do)
down the street (more difficult—
the street, a sort of means to an end,
something like a conveyor belt).
I noticed the sun (you know
that orange ball in the sky)...
oh, hell, I can't be explaining everything.
I'll give you the news, you'll have to take it
however you can get it and good luck.

That's how I felt
when I saw the sun this morning.
Good luck! I said to the world
filled with roads and one little man
who knows how to waltz. And bam,
when I said it I flung a spare
exclamation point down on the spot.
I leave these exclamation points as signs
of what little vigor may be left.

What with entropy, Bill Stubbs,
you'd say there's plenty
of loose energy but no and I don't know
where it goes to, just oozes away
so like I said bam! Another exclamation point
out of my pocket and onto the ground
and me waltzing up the road
like a cardboard box bounding up a conveyer
and the orange sun and you out there
a long way off on Uranus probably cold as hell.

ALBERT EINSTEIN AND THE WAVES
ROLLING INTO THE SEA

Even without the proof of the sun, even without
men in shoes walking through jungles, cameras,
and rounds of debate between lords
and gentlemen in large rooms, even so,
Einstein found his way in time.
Another asked him what if light didn't bend
when passing the sun what
then? And Einstein, "In that case I can only pity
the Good Lord for the theory is correct" and light
like many small songbirds came fluttering in
and bent around his body.
He pulled his hair away from his face,
checked his pockets for teeth or a comb, waved
his muscular hands through the air and the air,
like a friend, waved back.

Look at the moon
and the tide on some beach.
Einstein could tell
Marx what he was thinking
and Marx like more light rolled in
crying yes, it is so and
so the carcass of the body called State,
the State like a used up theory
bent in all directions at once
invoking God, good sense, the morality
of the ten blue angels
until the man again, but can you tell us,
Einstein, what will happen? And Einstein,
like a songbird repeating, what will happen?
to Marx what will happen?
until daybreak and the moon sets, the tides

going in or out, the men in jungles
with their shoes on their heads, saying
actually they're light but if we sink
crossing rivers what will happen? And the songbirds
carry them like waves carry themselves,
into the sea.

THINGS

This is the throwing out of all things,
the throwing out of dull objects and hardware,
the throwing out of the jigsaw puzzle of dust,
the throwing out of vegetable seeds that grow pineapples,
    of hemlock, pine, spruce and fir,
the throwing out also of concrete, steel, adobe, foam,
the throwing out of the dental equipment with the dental schools,
the throwing out of postcards,
the throwing out of Brussels and Rome,
the throwing out of all the islands of Fiji,
the throwing out of tulips,
the throwing out of DDT, 245T, Dieldrin,
the throwing out of the mountains,
the throwing out of the seashore,
the throwing out of the police.

Yes, this is the throwing out of all the things,
the throwing out of Hitler and Gandhi, Mussolini and Gramsci,
    Franklin Roosevelt and Norman Thomas, Erasmus and Confucius,
    the Shah of Iran and the Little Prince, Madame Bovary and
    Simone de Beauvoir,
the throwing out of compost and mulch,
the throwing out of the bathwater,
the throwing out of lentils, cornmeal, tofu,
the throwing out of abstract nouns,
the throwing out of the calendar,
the throwing out of board games and playing cards,
the throwing out of good weather,
the throwing out of the rings and bracelets and hats,
the throwing out of dumptrucks and backhoes.

Even I am beginning to believe
this is the throwing out of everything,

the throwing out of city streets,
the throwing out of waxwings, juncos, grosbeaks, gulls,
the throwing out of the binoculars to watch them,
the throwing out of the dead end sign at the end of my road,
the throwing out of the trailer house full of children,
the throwing out of the walls of the house next door,
the throwing out of my house,
the throwing out of my friends,
the throwing out of myself,
the throwing out of art and music, everything
thrown out, now writing.

LAST NIGHT ON EARTH

My last night on earth should be ordinary and plain
as a bus ride home, a refrigerator door, a tree.

Here is my room, not too dirty,
not too clean, not at all worn out, well broken in.

My shoes all fit, the brown and the black,
the green ones. I don't have shoes that don't fit.

I've got this tiny emerald ring, green
and light. I've got cats in a tree.

The gray sky, the blue sky, the low sky
filled with clouds, the memory of large machines.

Once I received a scented letter from a lover
long gone. Once I could be sad and torn like a leaf.

This horse is galloping on without me, can you
see it? I can see you know how to ride.

Here then is a post and there a charred piece of a spoon.
The wind blows and then it doesn't.

Moon is David Romtvedt's first book length collection of poetry. This paperback edition was lithographically reproduced from proofs of a clothbound limited edition hand printed at The Bieler Press of St Paul, Minnesota.

This book has been printed on acid-free paper & machine sewn to ensure durability and quality of production.